AN INSPECTOR CALLS: 12 AQA GCSE ENGLISH LITERATURE A STAR EXAM ANSWERS

Full mark A Star (Grade 9) Answers

By Joseph Anthony Campbell

CONTENTS

THE QUALITY CONTROL SYSTEM™ OR HOW TO GET AN A STAR!

The Quality Control System™ is fourfold.

It involves:

1) An efficient summary of the examination paper.

2) A concise focus upon the Assessment Objectives in the exam and how to approach them.

3) Clear instructions on your timings and how long you should spend on each question. ***This is the most important point of fact in this fourfold system***.

4) Further to point 3, the approximate word count per mark you should be consistently aiming for in each minute of your exam.

My students have applied all of the techniques of the Quality Control System™ I am providing you with to gain A stars (Grade 9's) in their examinations. You can replicate them by following the advice in this book. Following these rules has ensured success for my students in English Literature and their other subjects and it will do for you too! The Quality Control System is explained more fully at the end of this book.

AQA ENGLISH LITERATURE GCSE – 'AN INSPECTOR CALLS' FORMAT

Modern prose/drama – 1 item. 30 marks (AO1, AO2, AO3).

We are looking in this book at the '**Modern prose/drama**' section and the '**An Inspector Calls**' option. There are 12 examples of Grade 9, A star essays in this book. You will have a choice of two questions on the exam paper. Only answer one question.

The following 12 questions and answers will help you to prepare your Grade 9 essays and to massively improve your practice for your exams as I have covered all of the characters in '**An Inspector Calls**' in this book and all of the major themes.

The best approach for a **Grade 9** is to spend 50 minutes on each question; 40 minutes writing and 10 minutes making notes, planning and checking your final answer for basic corrections at the end of the examination.

This series of books have helped thousands of readers to achieve their potential!

AN INSPECTOR CALLS FIRST ESSAY – MR BIRLING

How does Priestley present the character of Mr Birling in <u>An Inspector Calls</u>?

Write about:

• *how Mr Birling responds to his family and to the Inspector*
• *how Priestley presents Mr Birling by the ways he writes.*

[30 Marks] (AO1 = 12; AO2 = 12; AO3 = 6) + AO4 = Spelling and Grammar [4 marks]

(50 Minutes Total = 40 Minutes Writing + 10 Minutes Making Notes/Planning/Checking Final Answer for Basic Corrections)

(600 Words Maximum per Essay = 15 Words per Minute)

Mr Birling is described by Priestley as, "heavy-looking," and "in his middle fifties". His wife, Sybil Birling, is his "social superior" according to Priestley and it is inferred that Mr Birling is from a more working-class background i.e., "rather provincial in his speech.". In the opening act of the play, he states that "...there isn't a chance of war" and that the Titanic is "unsinkable". Here, his arrogance and complacency are made very clear. He also views his daughter's engagement as a chance to push for "...lower costs and higher prices". He does not consider the impact "higher prices" might have on anyone else.

Mr Birling is the first to be interrogated by the Inspector. He remains unaffected by the details of the suicide, stating "(rather impatiently) Yes, yes. Horrid business.". This use of stage directions by Priestley reflects how Mr Birling is trying to control the timeframe of the present situation and conclude the investigation. The pace of the drama is controlled by Priestley who varies both the levels of fluency and the length of the dialogue. This ensures that the intended tone of the scene is preserved. Mr Birlings main concern appears to be avoiding "scandal," a word he is the only character to use and which he states a total of 7 times in the play. Priestley uses interruptions to further add to the drama, "(cutting in) Just a minute, Sheila.". This interruption shows that Mr Birling is afraid that his daughter is going to increase the chances of a "scandal".

When Mr Birling details Eva Smiths request for "more money" he shows his arrogance by suggesting reverentially that it is "...my duty to keep labour costs down" before stating to the Inspector, "So, I refused". This is a short, sharp, staccato sentence, dismissive of both the former requests of his employees and the Inspector and his investigation. Mr Birling claims to have sacked Eva Smith in an attempt to quell dissent amongst his employees. He is shown to be a man who will try to avoid taking any responsibility for his actions, responding to the Inspector with finality, "I can't accept any responsibility".

In how Mr Birling responds to his family, Priestley exemplifies Mr Birling's ignorance and pomposity through his ageism and sexism. Mr Birling lacks an understanding of the younger generation, reflected when he states that, "...so many of you don't seem to understand now". He thereby separates himself from the ("you") younger generation who do not have the capacity to understand what only he can. His attitude to women is also conveyed, when he states that they will "...join the ladies. That'll stop me giving you good advice". This point infers that only men could possibly understand his self-declared "good advice". When Gerald presents the idea that the Inspector is a fraudulent imposter, Mr Birling is delighted at his exoneration and the avoidance of a "public scandal", saying to Sheila "ask Gerald for that ring you gave back to him" (mainly perhaps in order to resume his potential merger with "Crofts Limited"). As a "...hard-headed businessman", he also insists that Eric reimburse him for the company money he stole. He is the epitome of a self-centred business owner.

Arthur Birling is an arrogant and dismissive character used by Priestley as a dramatic vehicle to personify capitalism, materialism and the self-satisfaction, pomposity and ignorance of the wealthy elder generation at the time the play was set. Mr Birling is, of course, not a human being with mental processes separate from those of the author and he is presented as a counterpoint to Priestley's own viewpoints.

(600 words)

AN INSPECTOR CALLS SECOND ESSAY – DIFFERENCES BETWEEN THE OLDER AND YOUNGER GENERATIONS

How does Priestley present some of the differences between the older and younger generations in <u>An Inspector Calls</u>?

Write about

• how the different generations respond to events and to each other
• how Priestley presents the different generations in the play.

[30 Marks] (AO1 = 12; AO2 = 12; AO3 = 6) + AO4 = Spelling and Grammar [4 marks]

(50 Minutes Total = 40 Minutes Writing + 10 Minutes Making Notes/Planning/Checking Final Answer for Basic Corrections)

(600 Words Maximum per Essay = 15 Words per Minute)

Priestley presents the different generations and their differences in 'An Inspector Calls'. Sheila and Eric Birling represent the younger generation whilst Mr and Mrs

Birling represent the older generation. Priestley presents the idea that there is hope in the younger generation and in their ability to learn from their mistakes and take responsibility for their actions and change. Contrastingly, the older characters' opinions and behaviours remain fixed and Mr Birling and Mrs Birling refuse to learn from their mistakes.

The older characters perceive Sheila and Eric as lacking the necessary social graces and understanding. Mrs Birling adheres to arbitrary social expectations as she admonishes Sheila for using the word "squiffy", stating, "What an expression, Sheila! Really, the things you girls pick up these days!". Mr Birling also states to Eric and Gerald, "But what so many of you don't seem to understand now" – referring to the younger men as "you" and how they "don't seem to understand". This exemplifies further Priestley's presentation of the differences between the older and younger generations, as Mr Birling, an older man, assumes that the younger generation are unable to grasp what he can.

Towards the end of the play, when Gerald suggests that the Inspector is a fraud, Mr and Mrs Birling are excited at the prospect that they could be fully exonerated. Mr Birling states of the Inspector that "...he behaved in a very peculiar and suspicious manner" and Mrs Birling supports him by stating, "His manner was quite extraordinary". However, Sheila and Eric are convinced that even if the Inspector was not a real Inspector and even if Eva Smith is alive, they are guilty of irresponsible and cruel actions. Eric even asserts himself when it becomes abundantly clear that his parents will not take responsibility for their actions against Eva Smith, "You're beginning to pretend now that nothing's really happened at all." Eric observes that his parents are trying to 'pretend' that nothing has happened when it is suggested that the Inspector was not real. He and Sheila, the younger characters, still feel responsible. Mr Birling also nearly attacks Eric physically. "Why, you hysterical young fool – get back – or I'll". Mr Birling implies here that Eric is a "fool" due to the fact that he is young. However, it is Arthur, who almost resorts to physical violence.

Through the Inspector's interrogation, the audience are permitted to understand more about each character and who they actually are and how the different generations respond to events and to each other. Sheila and Eric's response to Eva's death is markedly contrasted with Mr and Mrs Birling's response to Eva's death. Sheila and Eric develop a sense of social responsibility during the course of the play and are ashamed about their involvement in this death, becoming desperate to make amends. However, Mr Birling and Mrs Birling choose not to accept this responsibility; their attitude remaining unchanged from the beginning of the play.

The differences between the older and younger generations that Priestley presents are clear in that Mr and Mrs Birling are both unmoved and unrepentant about their involvement in Eva's death. The older generation are presented in a more negative light by Priestley, as unwilling and unable to learn from their mistakes. However, Sheila and Eric, as the younger generation, understand the Inspector's final message; and both admit their faults and repent of their actions. Attitudes towards responsibility may possibly contrast with what a contemporary audience reception's response would be yet at the time of the play's production, Priestley presents Eric and Sheila as providing a tentative hope of a brighter future.

(600 words)

By Joseph Anthony Campbell

AN INSPECTOR CALLS THIRD ESSAY – GERALD

How does Priestley present the character of Gerald in <u>An Inspector Calls</u>?

Write about:

• how Gerald responds to the Birling family and to the Inspector
• how Priestley presents Gerald by the ways he writes.

[30 Marks] (AO1 = 12; AO2 = 12; AO3 = 6) + AO4 = Spelling and Grammar [4 marks]

(50 Minutes Total = 40 Minutes Writing + 10 Minutes Making Notes/Planning/Checking Final Answer for Basic Corrections)

(600 Words Maximum per Essay = 15 Words per Minute)

Priestley presents different aspects of Gerald Croft's character in each of the three acts. Gerald is from an upper-class family who own "Crofts Limited". Gerald is described by Priestley as "an attractive chap about thirty, the easy well-bred young man-about-town". At the opening of the play, Gerald exudes confidence and charm. He is at the Birlings' home to celebrate his engagement to Sheila. He behaves like a member of the family with the Birlings', stating early on in the play "(smiling)... I insist upon being one of the family now.". When the Inspector's arrival is announced, Gerald even makes a gentle joke at Eric's expense to Mr Birling, as to why the

Inspector is there, that is especially ironic in hindsight, "...unless Eric's been up to something.". During the interrogation of Mr Birling, Gerald fervently supports him stating, "You couldn't have done anything else" and "I should say so!". He also attempts to control the Inspector's inquiry by stating, "I'd like to have a look at that photograph now, Inspector.". However, when the name, "Daisy Renton" is revealed, Priestley presents Gerald's shock, "(startled) What?". He is then evasive with Sheila, presented through an abrupt line of dialogue, "All right. I knew her. Let's leave it at that."

During the Inspector's interrogation, in the second act, Gerald states to Sheila, "You've been through it - and now". Priestley's use of a dramatic pause in the dialogue, through the use of a dash, heightens the vehemence of the line's delivery. However, Gerald quickly becomes conciliatory in tone, "No, no, I didn't mean", conveyed through Priestley's use of repetition. As Act 2 develops, Gerald redeems himself to some extent, through being more open and honest about his actions to Sheila and to the Inspector. Gerald tells the truth to the Inspector of how he met Daisy Renton and how she "gave... a glance that was nothing less than a cry for help.". Gerald no longer attempts to withhold information from the Inspector. This difference is quite discernible from his attitude in the first act, as he outlines the full extent of his involvement, "...when we met again - not accidentally this time of course". He also details how he "made her take some money" and that he "was sorry for her". Here, Priestley has Gerald use emotive language and this helps the audience view Gerald more positively. Sheila also commends Gerald for his honesty and his initial compassion for Daisy.

However, in the third act, Gerald turns sleuth and states that Goole was not a real police inspector, speculates as to whether they were all referring to the same woman and whether any girl killed herself at all. Although his initial suspicions appear confirmed, he also appears oblivious to any lack of morality he or the Birlings' have displayed, in the way they treat young women. Similar to Mr and Mrs Birling, he takes no responsibility for his actions, unlike his former fiancé Sheila and Eric.

Priestley uses the character of Gerald as a dramatic vehicle to reflect the upper-classes. Despite Gerald's pleasant appearance and manner, being both an "attractive chap" and "well-bred", he is still the executor of morally questionable behaviour. His idea of gentlemanly chivalry is exposed as a lie. He is evasive, dishonest and irresponsible. This is shown through his having an affair, attempting to conceal it and in his sudden dismissal of Daisy Renton. In the third act, Gerald is inferred by Priestley to believe that he is above moral reproach as he attempts to exonerate himself and the Birling family. Ultimately, he learns nothing from the Inspector's interrogation.

(600 words)

AN INSPECTOR CALLS FOURTH ESSAY – GENDER

How does Priestley explore the theme of gender in __An Inspector Calls__?

Write about:

• the ideas presented about the theme of gender in __An Inspector Calls__
• how Priestley presents these ideas about the theme of gender by the ways he writes.

[30 Marks] (AO1 = 12; AO2 = 12; AO3 = 6) + AO4 = Spelling and Grammar [4 marks]

(50 Minutes Total = 40 Minutes Writing + 10 Minutes Making Notes/Planning/Checking Final Answer for Basic Corrections)

(600 Words Maximum per Essay = 15 Words per Minute)

The theme of gender is explored in 'An Inspector Calls' which was first performed in 1945 at a time of great social change. During 'World War Two', women had a more prominent role in the workplace. This helped change existing stereotypical perceptions as regards ideas about the roles of women. Priestley also explores the impact of gender roles through the independence of Eva Smith. Eva Smith is a pivotal character that drives the plot. She is independent and stands up for her own rights and for the rights of others. Eva Smith is portrayed as an independent and outspoken young woman before her death and due to the predominant views as regards the roles of women coupled with societal expectations at this time – this could be viewed as both unusual and courageous.

Priestley also explores the theme of gender through the attitudes of Mr Birling and Gerald Croft and through the ways they view women. Mr Birling is patronising as regards his viewpoints upon women, believing that they cannot organise a proper strike and makes stereotypical statements about women as a whole. Mrs Birling also fulfils an old-fashioned female role through her attitudes towards marriage, as in her view, married women should fully support their husbands and not contradict them. Mrs Birling also judges Eva Smith extremely harshly because she is going to be a single mother.

In 'An Inspector Calls' Priestley explores and presents these ideas about the theme of gender through how he writes. When Mr Birling is instructing Eric and Gerald about women's attitudes towards the clothes they wear "...not only something to make 'em look prettier – but – well, a sort of sign or token of their self-respect" he shows that he has a patronising view of women, arrogantly assuming that he knows that clothes are a sign of self-respect for them. He has a stereotypical view of women and does not view them as individuals but suggests that all women are the same, referring to them simply as 'ladies', "...we'll join the ladies. That'll stop me giving you good advice". As Mr Birling makes these speeches removed from both his wife and daughter, this illustrates his attitude towards gender further; he views this as an exclusive talk for men only.

Gerald Croft also makes sexist comments about women from the bar he frequented. "I hate those hard-eyed dough-faced women." This masculine language and forceful hyperbolic phrasing are intended to suggest superiority and strength. Gerald is judgemental of how the women look, and thus he dislikes them. His romantic idea of gentlemanly chivalry towards a woman in distress may also be based principally on male lust and also presents themes of male ownership and Daisy Renton's lack of power. This might be perceived by the audience as ungentlemanly or even as sexual exploitation of the weak by the powerful.

Ideas about men and masculinity are presented by Priestley through how the male characters behave towards the females in the play. This highlights important points on gender and inequality and thus Priestley gives us a glimpse of the patriarchal society of the time. However, Mrs Birling also treats Eva Smith with contempt and cruelty, stating that Eva Smith is incapable of "...elaborate fine feelings and scruples that were simply absurd in a girl in her position.". Mrs Birling shows no empathy or compassion for another woman.

Although there would be a contrasting contemporary audience reception compared to a modern audience reception, it appears clear that Priestley intended that by the culmination of the play, the audience would have questioned their views of stereotypical gender roles.

(600 words)

By Joseph Anthony Campbell

AN INSPECTOR CALLS FIFTH ESSAY – MRS BIRLING

How does Priestley present the character of Mrs Birling in __An Inspector Calls__?

Write about:

• *how Mrs Birling responds to her family and to the Inspector*
• *how Priestley presents Mrs Birling by the ways he writes.*

[30 Marks] (AO1 = 12; AO2 = 12; AO3 = 6) + AO4 = Spelling and Grammar [4 marks]

(50 Minutes Total = 40 Minutes Writing + 10 Minutes Making Notes/Planning/Checking Final Answer for Basic Corrections)

(600 Words Maximum per Essay = 15 Words per Minute)

Priestley describes Mrs Birling as "...a rather cold woman and her husband's social superior". From the outset of the play, she is cold-hearted and condescending despite being the leader of a charitable organisation.

Throughout the dinner she chastises her family when they say or do things that she considers impolite. She views both Eric and Sheila as children, not as a young man or woman. When Sheila uses the word, "squiffy", Mrs Birling admonishes her, "What an expression, Sheila! Really, the things you girls pick up these days!". Mrs Birling also

16

maintains a state of denial to protect her family's reputation. This is exemplified when the Inspector suggests that Eric is used to drinking and Mrs Birling responds, "...of course not. He's only a boy." Her shock at the revelation from Sheila as regards Eric's habitual drinking is expressed through Priestley's presentation of a stage direction that states that Mrs Birling is "(staggered)", which is further evidence of her state of denial. However, she clearly approves of Gerald Croft and his social standing. This demonstrates Mrs Birling's sense of social superiority and the expectations she places on others to maintain her arbitrary standards.

Mrs Birling's coldness and sense of social superiority is evident throughout the play, particularly in her interactions with the Inspector. She even brazenly lies and denies that she recognises the girl's picture, "No. Why should I?". Mrs Birling even attempts to intimidate the Inspector, stating, "You know of course that my husband was Lord Mayor only two years ago". Priestley presents Mrs Birling as a sinister and cunning character who assumes a social and moral superiority over Inspector Goole, who she refers to as "impertinent" and "offensive".

Mrs Birling derides working class women like Eva as immoral, dishonest, and unprincipled. "She was claiming elaborate fine feelings and scruples that were simply absurd in a girl in her position.". Mrs Birling displays no compassion for Eva Smith as she explains her decision to refuse her claim for help. "So, I was perfectly justified in advising my committee not to allow her claim for assistance." Despite hearing about all the misfortune that Eva Smith has suffered, Mrs Birling is completely unmoved and without any empathy. There is a clear sense of irony as Mrs Birling is unaware that the unborn child would have been her own grandchild and she also states that if the father "...didn't belong to her class" then "...that's all the more reason why he shouldn't escape". Mrs Birling also unknowingly condemns her own son, Eric, who is the father of Eva Smith's child, "If the girl's death is due to anybody, then it's due to him."

Mrs Birling learns nothing from the Inspectors moral lessons and concluding speech. Mrs Birling states of the Inspector; incredulously, "The rude way he spoke to Mr Birling and me – it was quite extraordinary!". There is no progression or realisation after the full extent of the revelations that she faces. She refuses to accept responsibility and unlike Eric and Sheila, there is no acceptance of her guilt or any self-acknowledgement of the part she played in contributing to Eva Smith's untimely end. Similar to her husband, she is more concerned with maintaining the family's reputation, which is shown in her loyalty to her husband's view of how the world works. This is exemplified when she states, "Now just be quiet so that your father can decide what we ought to do." And the stage direction, "(Looks expectantly at Birling.)". Her delight at the irreality of the Inspector however, would have quickly turned to despair when the final phone-call is made.

(600 words)

AN INSPECTOR CALLS SIXTH ESSAY – HOW THE INSPECTOR SUGGESTS WAYS THAT SOCIETY COULD BE IMPROVED

How does Priestley use the character of the Inspector to suggest ways that society could be improved?

Write about:

• *what society is shown to be like in the play and how it might be improved*
• *how Priestley presents society through what the Inspector says and does.*

[30 Marks] (AO1 = 12; AO2 = 12; AO3 = 6) + AO4 = Spelling and Grammar [4 marks]

(50 Minutes Total = 40 Minutes Writing + 10 Minutes Making Notes/Planning/Checking Final Answer for Basic Corrections)

(600 Words Maximum per Essay = 15 Words per Minute)

Before the Inspector's arrival, Mr Birling claims that "...there isn't a chance of war" and that the Titanic is "unsinkable" which are heavily ironic references. Unlike Mr

Birling, Inspector Goole is a trustworthy character and emphasises Priestley's views. The author voices his opinions throughout the play, through the actions of his creation, Inspector Goole. The Inspector sheds a light on all the concerns that Priestley had at the time of writing 'An Inspector Calls' as regards societal improvement.

The stage directions for when the Inspector is first introduced, establish his powerful impact and presence as he is described as transmitting an, "...impression of massiveness, solidity and purposefulness". His entrance brings a strong change to the atmosphere of the Birlings' dining room, turning the slow, relatively peaceful pace into a tense and uneasy atmosphere. The Inspector's opening remarks are blunt and purposeful, "Two hours ago, a young woman died in the infirmary...she'd swallowed a lot of strong disinfectant." And then, he adds, with an almost casual sense of pathos, "Burnt her inside out, of course." There are varied reactions from the family and Gerald to the Inspector and they represent a macrocosm of the upper and middle classes, thus showing what 'society' is shown to be like in the play.

The Inspector investigates each family member individually and in doing so, reveals the consequences of their irresponsible and cruel behaviour. Priestley uses the Inspector to comment on society and how it is organised through Priestley's references to labour agitation, unfair wages and capitalism. Thus, Priestley presents society through what the Inspector says and does and how it might be improved. When the Inspector is questioning the Birlings he states, citing Eva Smith's appeal for higher wages, "It's better to ask for the earth than to take it". The Inspector infers that it is socially detrimental to "take" without permission. To "take" is what the Birlings and Gerald Croft habitually did, particularly in regards to Eva Smith.

The Inspector's final speech is a moral speech and the Inspector's use of language aids Priestley in conveying his message, (which revolves around the improvement of our society), to both the audience and the other characters of the play, "...there are millions and millions and millions of Eva Smiths". The repetition of "millions" emphasises his point that Eva is representative of many others and a part of the society in which they, and we, live, "...their lives, their hopes and fears ... all intertwined with our lives". These words enable the audience to empathise with Eva Smith.

Priestley uses the events of the play and the character of the Inspector to state that, "We are responsible for each other" and that if we do not learn this, that we, "...will be taught it in fire and blood and anguish." This is a biblical, terrifying and apocalyptic image which could be linked to the two world wars that occurred from when the play was set to when it was performed.

Ultimately, the Inspector teaches a number of lessons about how we should be responsible for each other and thus improve society. Priestley does, however, present the possibility of change through the younger generation and the characters of Eric and Sheila. He also uses the Inspector to make the audience question their own behaviour and morality and hopes that they will take heed of the Inspectors message to improve our sense of social responsibility and to improve the society we are a part of. The Inspector's final warning to the characters is therefore of equal relevance to both the characters of the play and a contemporary audience.

(600 words)

AN INSPECTOR CALLS SEVENTH ESSAY – SHEILA

How and why does Sheila change in <u>An Inspector Calls</u>?

Write about:

**• *how Sheila responds to her family and to the Inspector*
• *how Priestley presents Sheila by the ways he writes*.**

[30 Marks] (AO1 = 12; AO2 = 12; AO3 = 6) + AO4 = Spelling and Grammar [4 marks]

(50 Minutes Total = 40 Minutes Writing + 10 Minutes Making Notes/Planning/Checking Final Answer for Basic Corrections)

(600 Words Maximum per Essay = 15 Words per Minute)

Sheila is initially presented by Priestley as a naive and self-centred young woman. Sheila is immature, subservient and keen to behave well; referring to her father as 'Daddy', "I'm sorry Daddy actually I was listening.". However, Priestley states that Sheila is "(rather distressed)" in his stage directions when the Inspector informs her of Eva Smith's death. She immediately shows remorse for her part in Eva's downfall with her attitude changing as the play develops. She develops a sense of maturity, particularly evident when she confronts Gerald about his affair, "...in some odd way, I rather respect you more than I've ever done before". We have the first indicator of her level of insight when she states "I knew there was something fishy about that time.

And now at least you've been honest". Sheila finds a sense of peace in her honesty and in taking responsibility for her actions. As an audience, we are made aware of the profound change that has taken place within Sheila when she says to Gerald, "You and I aren't the same people who sat down to dinner here". She also respects Gerald's honesty, and the change she has seen in him. Becoming more assertive with her family, she encourages her family to take responsibility, "...so confident, so pleased with ourselves until he began asking us questions" and to realise that their actions can have grave consequences; yet her parents remain unmoved.

Priestley's stage direction, "half playful, half serious" when Sheila says to Gerald "...so you be careful" provides an ambiguous tone and adds more depth to the character of Sheila. Priestley's dramatic intention in providing this stage direction is to hint at an unresolved issue in Sheila and Gerald's relationship. Sheila later states, "Because I was in a furious temper" when explaining her behaviour towards Eva Smith. Sheila demonstrates her honesty here as she simply presents the facts.

Sheila demonstrates throughout the play that she is insightful and intelligent. Sheila discerns realities as regards the Inspector that the other characters cannot. Sheila uses the metaphor of a wall that the Inspector will demolish as she develops a keen insight into his methods. "I talked about building up a wall that's sure to be knocked flat." A change in Sheila is apparent here as the other characters do not realise this truth, as she states to her mother, "Go on, Mother. You might as well admit it" and to Gerald, "Of course he knows...You'll see.". By the end of the play, she has become more assertive, using phrases such as 'I tell you', which demonstrates the dramatic change in her character, "I tell you - whoever that inspector was, it was anything but a joke.". Priestley varies the length of the lines Sheila delivers and the pace of the drama is controlled by Priestley through his variation of the length and fluency of Sheila's lines.

Priestley uses Sheila's character to share his opinions on the contemporary youth of the time and to present the attitudes of a younger generation. Priestley presents a sense of hope in the young people of post-war Britain. Sheila changes throughout the play and distances herself from the selfish behaviour and capitalist views of her parents. This is clearly evident in how she is deeply affected by Eva Smith's death and feels a deep sense of remorse and is both ashamed and filled with guilt for her part in contributing to Eva's untimely demise. Through the Inspector, Sheila is changed and her social conscience is awakened. This profound level of change within her creates a new awareness of her responsibilities to others.

(600 words)

AN INSPECTOR CALLS EIGHTH ESSAY –RESPONSIBILITY

How does Priestley explore responsibility in <u>An Inspector Calls</u>?

Write about:

• *the ideas about responsibility in <u>An Inspector Calls</u>*
• *how Priestley presents these ideas by the ways he writes.*

[30 Marks] (AO1 = 12; AO2 = 12; AO3 = 6) + AO4 = Spelling and Grammar [4 marks]

(50 Minutes Total = 40 Minutes Writing + 10 Minutes Making Notes/Planning/Checking Final Answer for Basic Corrections)

(600 Words Maximum per Essay = 15 Words per Minute)

Throughout the play, the principal characters have differing attitudes towards the idea of responsibility. There is a discernible difference between the older and younger generations' response. Mr and Mrs Birling do not develop any sense of responsibility as regards their part in Eva Smith's death whereas Sheila and Eric develop a sense of responsibility throughout the course of the play. Priestley uses the characters' dialogue to reveal their awareness of their selfishness and the degree to which they feel responsible.

Sheila feels responsible and remorseful when she realises how she treated Eva Smith, saying to Gerald, "...I'm trying to tell the truth.". Eric also takes responsibility for his actions in the final act of the play, as he declares to his parents, "You lot may be letting yourselves out nicely, but I can't.". Whilst Gerald and Eric's parents are enjoying potential exoneration, Eric reflects upon the seriousness of his actions towards Eva. Contrastingly, Mrs Birling refuses to take any responsibility for the death of Eva Smith, instead deflecting blame to Eric and emphatically stating, "I'm absolutely ashamed of you.".

It is, however, through the character of Mr Birling, an archetypal capitalist, that Priestley most fully explores the idea of responsibility and the impact a lack of social responsibility can have on society. Priestley reflects this idea through his writing. He uses the pivotal character of Mr Birling to drive the plot and set the scene. Mr Birling states, "...a man has to make his own way – has to look after himself". His use of masculine language and forceful hyperbolic phrasing, attempts to convey strength. Mr Birling is an individualist who dismisses the principles of responsibility for one another and dismisses the socialist metaphorical imagery of humans being, "...like bees in a hive". Priestley's placing of this conversation early in the play suggests its key significance as the plot unfolds.

Priestley uses dramatic irony to great effect in the play. The Inspector's arrival is a dramatic device that serves as an interruption to Mr Birlings speech. The Inspector's purpose is to demonstrate how we should be and feel responsible for one another. The Inspector exposes each character's selfishness and the tragic effects that this has on Eva Smith. However, Mr Birling does not feel responsible for this, stating to the Inspector that, "If we were all responsible for everything that happened to everybody we'd had anything to do with, it would be very awkward, wouldn't it?". Mr Birling's language highlights the power dynamic in this conversation and his use of rhetoric is manipulative. Mr Birlings' viewpoint is diametrically opposed to Priestley's views on social responsibility.

Mr and Mrs Birling and Gerald remain callous and unchanged, despite being made aware of their irresponsible and cold actions towards Eva Smith. Eric and Sheila do become aware, in hindsight, of the gravity of their actions against Eva Smith and take their share of responsibility. However, Eva Smith dies because no character takes responsibility for their actions against her at the time that they were performed and Priestley uses this fact to make important points about society and responsibility.

Priestley treats the idea of responsibility as a social issue. During the early 20th-century, there was no government support for the poor and Priestley wanted his audience to be both responsible for their own behaviour and for the welfare of others. The tragic consequences of the Birlings' actions highlight Priestley's ideas on responsibility. Through the death of Eva Smith, who is but one in, "millions", she serves as a metaphor to add greater weight to Priestley's fundamental question: Are we responsible for one another in society?

(600 words)

AN INSPECTOR CALLS NINTH ESSAY – ERIC

How far does Priestley present Eric as a character who changes his attitudes towards himself and others during the play?

Write about:

• *what Eric says and does throughout the play*
• *how far Priestley presents Eric as a character who changes his attitudes.*

[30 Marks] (AO1 = 12; AO2 = 12; AO3 = 6) + AO4 = Spelling and Grammar [4 marks]

(50 Minutes Total = 40 Minutes Writing + 10 Minutes Making Notes/Planning/Checking Final Answer for Basic Corrections)

(600 Words Maximum per Essay = 15 Words per Minute)

Eric's nervousness and lack of confidence is presented by Priestley at the outset of the play. Eric is in his early twenties and Priestley describes him in the stage directions as, "...not quite at ease, half shy, half assertive". Eric is unsure of himself, which is manifested in his awkward and stilted speech which Priestley presents through Eric's sudden outburst. "I don't know - really. Suddenly I felt I just had to laugh." At this point in the play, Eric delivers his lines with pauses and breaks in them and he cannot explain his sudden desire to laugh. Priestley also presents repetition in Eric's dialogue when referring to his father's dismissal of Eva Smith, "He could. He could have kept her on instead of throwing her out." Priestley's use of this technique provides an extra dimension of realism to Eric through his dialogue. This example of repetition presents Eric's uncertainty and hesitancy and conveys the subtleties of Eric's character.

There are moments in the play when Eric attempts to be assertive and to present his point of view through a well-reasoned argument with his father, as shown by Priestley when Eric questions his father's decision to dismiss Eva Smith. "And I don't see why she should have been sacked just because she'd a bit more spirit than the others.". However, his father dismisses Eric's views in their entirety. Eric is presented by Priestley as distanced from the other members of his family and as an isolated character, both ill at ease with himself and others.

Eric's social class appears to have shielded him from the consequences of both his excessive drinking and his casual relationships with women. However, Priestley shows the dramatic consequences that can result from such behaviour, in the final act of the play, through Eric's account of his relationship with Eva and the revelation of his feelings for and behaviour towards her. Eric is presented as an irresponsible drunk, which led to his physically forcing himself upon Eva and getting her pregnant. This shameful revelation culminates with both himself and his family realising the gruesome fact that Eva Smith was pregnant with Eric's baby when she committed suicide.

It is, however, after the Inspector exits the stage that Priestley presents Eric as a character who changes his attitudes towards himself and others. Eric's experiences with the Inspector appear to have created a seismic shift in his attitude. This is evidenced through Priestley's presentation of the change in his behaviour with his parents. He assertively states, "(bursting out) ... You're beginning to pretend now that nothing's really happened at all." He then states the stark and emotionally affecting fact that Eva's "...still dead". He, unlike his parents, fully understands the gravity of the situation, "I did what I did. And mother did what she did. And the rest of you did what you did to her." His use of repetition here adds emphasis and displays the clarity of his understanding of the situation. He is completely honest about the wrongs he has done, "I stole some money, Gerald, you might as well know" and he finally confronts and dismisses his father's attempts at further dishonesty "(As Birling tries to interrupt.) I don't care, let him know". Erics blunt yet compassionate speech is almost reminiscent of the Inspector.

Priestley presents Eric's shift in his attitude towards himself and others through his growing assertiveness and through his repentance and his full acceptance of the way he mistreated Eva Smith. Through Eric, Priestley infers that the new generation of a post-war Britain may point the way towards a more hopeful future.

(600 words)

AN INSPECTOR CALLS TENTH ESSAY – SOCIAL CLASS

How does Priestley explore the importance of social class in __An Inspector Calls__?

Write about:

• some ideas about social class in the play
• how Priestley presents the importance of social class.

[30 Marks] (AO1 = 12; AO2 = 12; AO3 = 6) + AO4 = Spelling and Grammar [4 marks]

(50 Minutes Total = 40 Minutes Writing + 10 Minutes Making Notes/Planning/Checking Final Answer for Basic Corrections)

(600 Words Maximum per Essay = 15 Words per Minute)

Priestley's presentation of the importance of social class is a key theme in 'An Inspector Calls'. From the outset of the play, the presentation of the character of Edna, who is the Birlings' maid, embodies the theme of the importance of social class. Edna represents a working-class member of the Birling household. Mr Birling states, "Edna'll answer it" when the Inspector visits the Birlings' house and then we hear her state, with expected reverence, "Please, sir, an Inspector's called." Later in the play, Mrs Birling states, "I asked her to wait up to make us some tea". Edna provides insight into the life of Eva Smith as they both share a working-class background. The presence of Edna indicates the luxury of the Birlings' lives and serves as a reminder of the Birlings' wealth and highlights ideas about social class.

Before the Inspector arrives, Mr Birling is pontificating upon socialist ideas, "...as if we were all mixed up together like bees in a hive - community and all that nonsense". Mr Birling's arrogance serves to communicate Priestley's contrasting views upon social class. Later, when questioned by the Inspector, Mr Birling comments on Eva's activism and Priestley uses this to reference the themes of labour agitation, unfair wage structures and the nature of capitalism. Two distinct social classes are represented by Mr Birling and Eva Smith; that of an upper class, wealthy factory owner and that of a poor, working-class woman.

Mrs Birling holds an extremely negative view of the working classes, "As if a girl of that sort would ever refuse money!" – referencing when Eva approached her charity for help. She believes that working-class girls collectively lack morality and have no principles. Mrs Birling has most likely never stopped to consider that she was simply born into the more prosperous side of the class equation. Her elitist views are further exemplified when Gerald details the behaviour of "Alderman" Joe Meggarty, "...a notorious womaniser" and "...one of the worst sots and rogues in Brumley." Mrs Birling replies "(staggered) well, really! Alderman Meggarty!". Priestley's use of stage directions indicates the level of shock she experiences. Priestley also critiques the notions of social superiority and hypocrisy that Mrs Birling's philanthropic efforts entail.

Priestley's presentation of Eva's decline into poverty and suicide, through the actions of the Birling family and Gerald Croft, reflects ideas as regards social class powerfully within the play. Priestley highlights the inequality between both upper and working-classes and what this demonstrates about the lives of the poor at this time. In the Inspector's final speech, Eva Smith is referred to as a representative of "millions" of vulnerable working-class people. Priestley presents ideas throughout the play as to how the lives of the poor might be improved and predates the creation of Britain's welfare state in 1948.

Priestley presents how Sheila and Eric become fully aware of their own selfishness and throughout the play he highlights the inequality between social classes that existed at the time the play was performed. In the first act of the play, we learn that Mr Birling dismissed Eva Smith after she asked for herself and others to have a wage rise. Mr Birling opines, "If you don't come down sharply on some of these people, they'd soon be asking for the earth." Priestley, through the character of the Inspector, states in his concluding speech, "We are members of one body. We are responsible for each other". Ultimately, Priestley's desire is for the audience not to see those of differing social classes as 'these people' but to realise instead, that we should all look after one another.

(600 words)

AN INSPECTOR CALLS ELEVENTH ESSAY – THE INSPECTOR

How does Priestley present the character of the Inspector in <u>An Inspector Calls</u>?

Write about:

• *how the Inspector responds to the other characters of the play*
• *how Priestley presents the Inspector by the ways he writes.*

[30 Marks] (AO1 = 12; AO2 = 12; AO3 = 6) + AO4 = Spelling and Grammar [4 marks]

(50 Minutes Total = 40 Minutes Writing + 10 Minutes Making Notes/Planning/Checking Final Answer for Basic Corrections)

(600 Words Maximum per Essay = 15 Words per Minute)

Priestley presents the Inspector as transmitting an, "impression of massiveness, solidity and purposefulness". His 'massiveness' combined with his 'purposefulness', convey that the Inspector is an imposing figure.

The Inspector arrives as the Birling family celebrate the engagement of Sheila Birling and Gerald Croft, stating, "I'd like some information, if you don't mind, Mr Birling. Two hours ago, a young woman died". His arrival transforms the slow and peaceful pace of the play and brings a sense of immediacy, whilst simultaneously creating a more tense and uneasy atmosphere. This is explained further through Priestley's notes on the stage lighting. "The lighting should be pink and intimate until the INSPECTOR arrives and then it should be brighter and harder". The lighting thus becomes a metaphorical interrogative flashlight for the characters of the play. The Inspector interrogates each character in turn and reveals the full consequences of their actions. The Inspector responds to the other characters of the play through interrupting them when they attempt to steer the conversation, and he thereby controls each interaction. This works to build suspense and tension throughout the play for the audience.

The Inspector is purposeful and pursues his objectives until they are completed. He obtains the information he needs from every character and exposes the failures in the other characters by revealing their crimes and wrongdoings, thus driving the drama forward. Both intelligent and powerful, he captures the full attention of the audience and directs the pace of the entire play, making his revelations specifically when they will have the most dramatic effect. He serves several dramatic functions within the play and he is also deeply mysterious, which adds a sense of intrigue to the play.

Priestley states in his character description that the Inspector has a "disconcerting habit of looking hard at the person he addresses before actually speaking.". This is displayed by Priestley at the end of the first act with the Inspector, "(looking steadily and searchingly at them.)". This also creates a dramatic pause in the action, as he states to Sheila and Gerald "Well?". The Inspector also uses emotionally affecting and shocking language as he describes Eva Smith's current state, "Her position now is that she lies with a burnt out inside on a slab.". However, it is perhaps, through Priestley's presentation of the Inspector's final speech, which acts as a warning of the consequences of moral irresponsibility, that the most affecting, apocalyptic and prophetic language is used, as they will be "...taught... in fire and blood and anguish.".

The Inspector has a profound impact upon the play. For example, there is a marked contrast in the attitudes of Eric and Sheila from when the Inspector first arrives to when he leaves. Priestley presents the Inspector as having a supernatural omniscience, and even his name, "Goole" is a homophone for the word "ghoul". Once he exits the stage, the other characters question his credentials and it is revealed that

Inspector Goole is not an actual police Inspector, which creates a deepening sense of mystery. Does Goole speak for Priestley's conscience? Does Priestley use the Inspector as a dramatic device to interrogate the conscience of the audience and provide them with a path of redemption from a future of "fire and blood and anguish"?

The final phone call in the play serves to reveal that a real investigation will follow Inspector Goole's. Although there could be a contrasting contemporary audience reception compared to a modern audience, perhaps Priestley also uses this phone call to pose the question of whether both the characters and the audience will now accept full responsibility for their wrongdoing?

(600 words)

AN INSPECTOR CALLS TWELFTH ESSAY – EVA SMITH

*How does Priestley present the character of Eva Smith in **An Inspector Calls**?*

Write about:

• how Eva Smith interacts with the Birling family and with Gerald
• how Priestley presents Eva Smith by the ways he writes.

[30 Marks] (AO1 = 12; AO2 = 12; AO3 = 6) + AO4 = Spelling and Grammar [4 marks]

(50 Minutes Total = 40 Minutes Writing + 10 Minutes Making Notes/Planning/Checking Final Answer for Basic Corrections)

(600 Words Maximum per Essay = 15 Words per Minute)

In the play, 'An Inspector Calls', the Inspector's investigation focuses on the death of Eva Smith. Eva Smith is a very significant character, despite not being present onstage throughout the play. Priestley presents the character of Eva Smith to the audience, through the Inspector, who has read both a letter and a diary that she kept, whilst she was alive. We never actually meet Eva Smith but we empathise with her as a character. It is through the Inspector that we get a sense of who she is and what happened to her. The Inspector begins his investigation in the opening act, stating, "I'd like some information...Two hours ago, a young woman died in the infirmary.". The fact that this is such a recent tragedy increases the levels of shock that the audience and the characters would feel. The gruesome details of Eva's death are expressed bluntly by the Inspector, "...swallowed a lot of strong disinfectant. Burnt her inside out, of course.". The details of her suicide are emotionally affecting to the audience, as is the level of pain that she experienced, as the Inspector continues to reveal the cold, horrific facts, "...she was in great agony... Suicide, of course." This adds to the dramatic impact of Eva's suicide, despite its occurrence being offstage.

Priestley presents Eva Smith evocatively throughout the play. As Eva is not present on the stage, much of the information about her must be inferred, as it is being related from a secondary source. Eva Smith interacts with all of the members of the Birling family and with Gerald. Perhaps somewhat surprisingly, when referring to Eva Smith, Mr Birling acknowledges her qualities, "A good worker too. In fact, the foreman there told me he was ready to promote her" before his opinion lessened of her when she, "...suddenly decided to ask for more money." Eva Smith displayed courage when she organised a strike for higher wages and Eric supports this view when he states, "I don't see why she should have been sacked". This is the beginning of Eva Smiths' downward decline as she loses her job as a factory worker and then another, more genteel job, in a clothes shop, through Sheila's intervention, when she, "...caught sight of this girl smiling... – and I was absolutely furious.".

Her relationship with Gerald, when she changes her name to Daisy Renton, reveals her emotional sensitivity. Through Eva's diary, the Inspector details how Eva Smith needed to be "quiet" and to "remember" after her love affair with Gerald. The distressing fact that she felt that "...there'd never be anything as good again for her" makes the audience realise the deep levels of sadness and reflectiveness that she felt when this relationship was ended by Gerald. The audience empathises with her and her emotional sensitivity is diametrically opposed to how Gerald simply and dishonestly resumed his life and former relationship with Sheila. By the time Eva meets Eric and Mrs Birling, her life has spiralled into grim desperation.

The Inspector never refrains from reminding the audience and the Birlings and Gerald of the gruesome, agonising and unnecessary death that Eva endured. In the Inspector's concluding speech, he states that there are "...millions of Eva Smiths" being exploited through the selfishness of others. Priestley uses the character of Eva

Smith to relate his beliefs about social responsibility, age, gender and class. The audience is invited to judge the behaviour of the offending characters within the play yet as an audience we are also forced to reflect upon our own behaviour and sense of morality, and upon how we treat others.

(600 words)

ASSESSMENT OBJECTIVES

There are **four assessment objectives** assessed in each English Literature examination: **AO1, (12 Marks) AO2 (12 Marks) AO3 (6 Marks) and AO4 (4 marks for Spelling and Grammar).**

AO1 = Read, understand and respond to text (An Inspector Calls) and the task set in the question. Use 4 to 6 quotations you may have memorised from the play (or memorise those that I have provided in my answers in this book on various characters/themes in the play).

AO2 = Analyse the language, form and structure used by a writer (Priestley) to create meanings and effects i.e., also mention 'Priestley' 4 to 6 times or more in your answer and how he presents characters/themes and creates meanings and effects.

AO3 = is the understanding of the relationship between the ideas in the text and the context/time in which the text was written and the context within which the text is set.

AO4 = spell and punctuate with consistent accuracy, and consistently use vocabulary and sentence structures to achieve control of the meaning you are aiming to convey.

The Assessment Objectives are not provided in the examination itself. However, I have provided which assessment objectives are being assessed in the practice questions in this book. It is important to be aware of the structure of how the assessment objectives are allocated in each question of the exam in order to maximise your opportunities to obtain full marks in each question.

TIMINGS

In the English Literature GCSE Paper 1 examination there are 60 marks to aim for in 1 hour and 40 minutes (100 minutes). Please allocate the correct words per minute per mark! Again, to re-iterate: The best approach is to spend 50 minutes on each question – 40 minutes writing and 10 minutes making notes, planning and checking your final answer for basic corrections at the end of the examination.

If you have extra time allocated to you, just change the calculation to accommodate the extra time you have i.e., if you have 25% extra time (= 50 minutes writing per question = 12 words per minute and 20 words per mark) and if you have 50% extra time (= 1 hour writing per question = 10 words per minute and 20 words per mark) also equals a 600-word essay for each section on Paper 1. Please **move on from the set question as soon as you have reached or are coming towards your time limit**. This ensures that you have excellent coverage of your whole exam and therefore attain a very good mark.

Similar to all the principles in this book, **you must apply and follow the correct timings for each question and stick to them throughout your exam to get an A star (Grade 9) in your English Literature examinations.** Without applying this principle in these examinations (and to a large extent all examinations) you cannot achieve the highest marks! **Apply all of the principles provided in this book to succeed!**

APPROXIMATE WORD COUNT PER QUESTION

Now that you know what is on each examination, how the assessment objectives are assessed and the time allocated for each type of question; we come to what would be considered the correct word count per mark for each question. The primary principle though is to spend the right amount of time on each question.

In the answers in this book, I have provided the maximum word count for each answer which works out at **15 words per minute and 20 words per mark and therefore this equals a 600-word essay for each section on Paper 1**. If your answer has quality, this gives you the very best chance of obtaining the highest marks in your English Literature exam. Obviously, it does not if you are waffling however. (Please remember to answer the question set and to move on in the time allocated.)

I am aware that some students can write faster than others but all should be able to write 10 words per minute and thus a 400-word essay in the time (if they have not been allocated extra time). This is where conciseness is important in your writing.

My students and readers have applied all of the techniques of the Quality Control System™ I am providing you with; to gain A stars (Grade 9's) in their examinations. You can replicate them by following the advice in this book.
Thank you for purchasing this book and best wishes for your examinations! Joseph

AUTHOR'S NOTE

This book will provide you with 12 crystal clear and accurate examples of 'A' star grade (Grade 9) AQA GCSE English Literature 'An Inspector Calls' answers from the 'Modern prose/drama' section of the new syllabus and enables students to achieve the same grade in their upcoming examinations.

I teach both GCSE and A level English and Psychology and I am a qualified and experienced teacher and tutor of over 19 years standing. I teach, write and provide independent tuition in central and west London.

The resources in this book WILL help you to get an A star (Grade 9) in your GCSE English Literature examinations, as they have done and will continue to do so, for my students.

Best wishes,

Joseph

ABOUT THE AUTHOR

I graduated from the Universities of Liverpool and Leeds and I obtained first class honours in my teacher training.

I have taught and provided private tuition for over 19 years up to university level. I also write academic resources for the Times Educational Supplement.

My tuition students, and now, my readers, have been fortunate enough to attain places to study at Oxford, Cambridge and Imperial College, London and other Russell Group Universities. The students have done very well in their examinations. I hope and know that my English Literature books can enable you to take the next step on your academic journey.

Printed in Great Britain
by Amazon

21772312R00026